HAIDA

Their Art and Culture

hancock

house

AUTHOR'S NOTE

Much of the information contained in this booklet is drawn from Part 1 of *Argillite: Art of the Haida*, by Leslie Drew and Douglas Wilson (Hancock House Publishers Ltd., 1980). In that text it was presented as background to the argillite carving art developed exclusively by the Haida. Supplementary material has been added, where appropriate, from the Newcombe papers, that invaluable and almost untapped source, now catalogued in the British Columbia Provincial Archives. My thanks to my Haida friend and associate Douglas Wilson, who checked these pages and made suggestions for the chapter dealing with the arts of the Haida in general.

HAIDA

Their Art and Culture

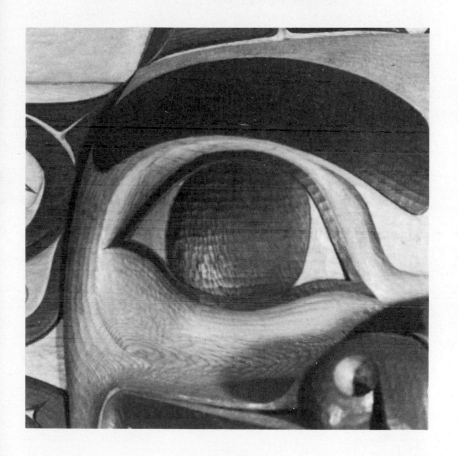

hancock

house

ISBN 0-88839-132-3

Copyright © 1982 Leslie Drew

Cataloging in Publication Data

Drew, Leslie
Haida, their art and culture

1. Haida Indians. 2. Haida Indians—Art.
3. Indians of North America—British Columbia
—Art. I. Title.
E99.H2D73   970.004'97   082-091166-6

Editor Margaret Campbell
Typeset by Lisa Smedman in Times Roman on an AM
 Varityper Comp/Edit
Layout Lisa Smedman
Production & Cover Design Peter Burakoff
Printed in Hong Kong

Paperback: Second Printing 1989

Hancock House Publishers Ltd.
19313 Zero Avenue, Surrey, B.C., Canada V3S 5J9
Hancock House Publishers
1431 Harrison Avenue, Blaine, WA 98230

CONTENTS

Skedans. Photo: G.M. Dawson, 1879. ➤

INTRODUCTION

The Haida are islanders first and foremost—a people apart. They are the native inhabitants of the Queen Charlotte Islands, a long, tooth-shaped archipelago lying off the northern coast of British Columbia. Exactly how long they have lived there is not known, but they had probably occupied the chain of islands for thousands of years before the white man discovered them.

Experts at building and navigating sea-going canoes, the Haida ranged far from their island stronghold, trading with, and sometimes raiding, the villages of their nearest neighbors—the Kwakiutl to the south, the Tsimshian across the often-stormy waters of Hecate Strait, and the Tlingit to the north in what is now part of Alaska. There are also Haida in Alaska, referred to as Kaigani Haida, descendants of a group who migrated from the Queen Charlotte Islands to Dall Island and Prince of Wales Island before the coming of the white man. The major Kaigani center today is Hydaburg, Alaska.

Haida villages once existed all around the two main islands of the Charlottes—Graham Island in the north and Moresby Island in the south—and on smaller islands in the chain. Rotting beams of houses and the toppled forms of giant cedar totem poles propped by new trees of a reassertive forest mark the ruins of several of these villages, and bear silent testimony to the decimation of the Haida. These once-thriving people were ravaged by disease and the effects of alcohol in the 1800s, after the whites arrived. From a population estimated at nearly 7,000 in 1835 (perhaps one-tenth of the total native population of what is now British Columbia), the Haida of the Charlottes dwindled to a mere 800 by 1885 and remained low in numbers into this century. Today, the two centers of population are the village of Haida, formerly called Old Masset, which has 1,000 people, and Skidegate, which has 400. Together, they make up nearly half the total population of the Charlottes. As well, an estimated 2,000 Haida reside elsewhere in British Columbia, many of them in Prince Rupert, Vancouver and Victoria. To all, the Queen Charlotte Islands are the homeland, the source of their distinctive culture, the inspiration for their arts.

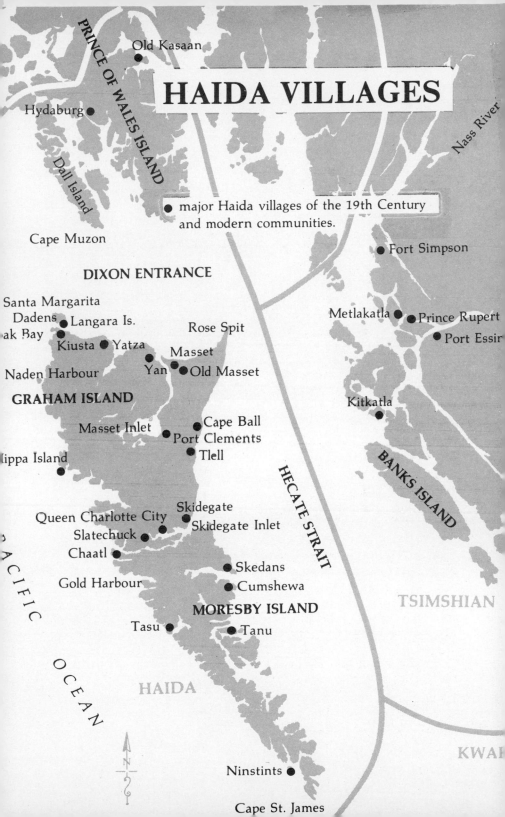

HAIDA VILLAGES

Old Kasaan

PRINCE OF WALES ISLAND

Hydaburg

Dall Island

Nass River

● major Haida villages of the 19th Century and modern communities.

Cape Muzon

Fort Simpson

DIXON ENTRANCE

Santa Margarita
Dadens ● Langara Is.
ak Bay
Kiusta ● Yatza

Rose Spit

Metlakatla ● ● Prince Rupert
● Port Essir

Naden Harbour

Yan ● Old Masset

Masset

GRAHAM ISLAND

Kitkatla

Masset Inlet

Cape Ball
Port Clements
● Tlell

lippa Island

BANKS ISLAND

Skidegate
Queen Charlotte City ●
Slatechuck
Chaatl ●

Skidegate Inlet

HECATE STRAIT

Skedans
Gold Harbour
Cumshewa

MORESBY ISLAND

TSIMSHIAN

Tasu ● ● Tanu

PACIFIC OCEAN

HAIDA

KWA

N

Ninstints ●

Cape St. James

Masset. Photo: G.M. Dawson, 1878.

Skidegate. Photo: G.M. Dawson, 1878.

Kaisun. Photo: C.F. Newcombe, 1901.

Skidegate.

Kung. Photo: G.M. Dawson, 1878.

Tanu, 1912.

B.C. Provincial Museum, Victoria
Neg. #PN5541

15

Cumshewa. Photo: G.M. Dawson, 1878.

Skedans. Photo: G.M. Dawson, 1878.

25

A LAND APART

The word *Haida* means simply "people"—people of the islands. This was a small nation unto itself, protected by forbidding seas. While the Haida had much in common culturally with their closest neighbors, the Tlingit and the Tsimshian, such as shared customs, corresponding social organizations, and trading links, geographically they were aloof, sea-buttressed, distinctive.

The climate of the Queen Charlotte Islands is mild and rainy, tempered by the warm Kuroshio current sweeping around the Pacific Rim. Yet while it may not be cold, the weather can be brutal and unpredictable. Storms can be fiercer here than anywhere else on the British Columbia coast. (A sustained wind velocity of S.S.E. 176 kilometers per hour was recorded at Cape St. James in October, 1963, calculated as gusting up to 237 kph.) After days of scudding black clouds and heavy rain will come a day of brilliant sunshine, bursting with a clarity like the dawn of creation. On days like these, mirages can be seen from the North Beach, outlined against the mountains of Alaska. Mystifying rose-tinted forms rise, flicker, and then fade under the changing skies.

Phenomena of a more permanent sort can be found the length and breadth of this grandly lonesome land. Far to the south, on a tiny island off Moresby Island, hot springs bubble and steam. (Haida elders welcome a chance to soak aching joints at this rustic spa.) The topography varies greatly. In some places, muskeg lowlands stretch into sand dunes and sweeping beaches; in other regions, deep inlets lined with rocky walls etch the landscape. From the central highlands, mountains snow-capped for most of the year rise to a height of 1,200 meters. The wave-pounded west coast is perhaps the most spectacular area of all. There, the mountains drop straight into the ocean. Newton Chittenden, exploring the Islands for the British Columbia government in 1884, asked about the seldom visited terrain. His Haida guide replied wryly: "There is no land, it is all mountains, forests, and water."

Peculiarities crop up in plant species. By the banks of the Yakoun River stands a golden spruce tree, a biological freak in color. Certain plants are found only on the Charlottes and nowhere else in the world, and some other plants differ greatly from their mainland counterparts. Some birds and mammals, too, are definitely different from their mainland family members, and some animals of

Coastline of the Queen Charlotte Islands.

the mainland were absent entirely. Deer and elk, for instance, are fairly modern introductions.

This, then, was the remote, diversified land that belonged to the Haida. Here on seashore strips near reliable freshwater streams, usually with dense forest as a backdrop, they built their villages and developed their culture. These were permanent settlements, as distinct from summer fishing camps. How many of these villages had risen and fallen by the time the white man came we do not know. But in the early 1800s nearly twenty groups of villages known by one or more names existed at places like Cape Ball, Rose Spit, Masset, and Kiusta in the north; Tanu, Skedans, Cumshewa, and Skidegate on the eastern and central coasts, and Tasu, Kaisun, Chaatl, and Anthony Island on the west coast.

A few villages were accessible one to the other by trail, but most only by sea. Viewed from offshore, these villages would be seen as a single row or parallel rows of long houses dressed with carved poles facing seaward and, at the beach, canoes of various sizes drawn up and ready for launching when the weather was right. The Haida had come to grips with their environment and in doing so had become a powerful, vigorous people.

21

A PEOPLE APART

The Haida were originally a dark-haired, dark-eyed people, though more than one observer noted that on the whole they were fairer in complexion than other northwest coast peoples. The first white traders to encounter them came in the summertime, taking care to avoid the perils their sailing ships faced in the late autumn gales. But the Haida spent their summers away from their permanent villages gathering food, especially fishing for halibut and salmon, so the first reports generally tell us little about the Haida themselves or of village life as it was lived normally—the homemaking, the customs, the rich ceremonials. Instead, we learn that canoeloads of Haida greeted the newcomers in song, welcomed them formally, marvelled at their ships and the ships' fittings, and proved to be keen, eager traders.

The Haida had long been exploiting their own resources to the full. From centuries of experience, they knew what to use and how to use it. They knew of all the teeming halibut banks, the streams alive with trout and spawning salmon, the prolific clam beds, the extensive bird colonies with their abundant supplies of eggs. They knew the best places, like Eden Lake, Juskatla, and Cumshewa Inlet, for selecting big cedars for canoe-making. They knew the finest berry patches, and the bogs yielding plants that made medicines. Using simple tools of stone and wood, they had built remarkably substantial family houses, had hollowed and shaped cedars for huge canoes, and had carved giant poles, raising them and their house beams with little more than sheer musclepower. The Haida and neighboring peoples did, however, have metal knives, some copper, and pieces of iron probably salvaged from the wreckage of Japanese vessels cast up on Pacific Northwest shores.

With the white man came iron tools in quantity, plus labor-saving mechanical devices such as the pulley, and the Haida were quick to make use of them. In the first barterings with whites, they were much more interested in receiving iron wedges than beads. Ever since, the Haida have been noted for seizing on technological advances, often adapting them immediately to their specific needs. In the same way, they pick up every new means of communication. This is the other, outgoing side to being an islander.

As for the Haida language itself, linguists today call this language an "isolate"—that is, one completely unrelated to any

Haida woman wearing labret.

other language, like that of the Basque of Europe and the Ainu of Japan. While it contains words borrowed from the Tsimshian and Tlingit, the basic vocabulary, at one time believed to be distantly related to Athapaskan, with which the Tlingit language is thought to be remotely linked, is now considered unique, neither sharing a vocabulary nor having an ancestral form in common with any other language in the world. Each village spoke its own dialect. Today, after consolidation, only the Masset and Skidegate dialects remain in the Charlottes, each fairly well understood in the other's village. The Kaigani also speak a Haida dialect. Many middle-aged and elderly Haida continue to speak the language in their homes and on Haida public occasions, and young people are being encouraged to learn it, although English predominates.

As well as their unifying language, the Haida had social, kinship, and inheritance systems in common. Thus, even though villages might be far apart, and feuds might blaze into open conflict between villages now and then, within the Islands the people formed a clearly-defined, homogeneous group. All were Haida and proud of it.

Significantly, the Haida made a very favorable impression on those early visitors who looked at them objectively. One was the Spanish naval officer Jacinto Caamano, sent north from New Spain on an exploratory journey. He commented that of all the Indians along the coast, one couldn't meet kinder people, more civilized in essentials or of better disposition. The year was 1792.

A Ninstints pole yields to nature.

THE WHITES COME

Geography—and a precious commodity—placed the Haida directly in the path of European exploration and exploitation. The first Europeans came in 1774. Juan Perez, in the *Santiago*, had been ordered by the viceroy of New Spain to search out whatever lay between present-day California and Cape St. Elias, at 60 degrees north latitude, then the southernmost limit of Russian exploration. Perez and his men first encountered Haida people at Langara (North) Island, and his naming of Cape Santa Margarita is the first European place-naming on record along the entire coast from Monterey to Cape St. Elias.

The first man to conduct serious trade with the Haida was England's George Dixon, who sailed into Haida waters in 1787 and named the islands after his ship, the *Queen Charlotte*. Dixon had served with the famous navigator-explorer James Cook on his third and final voyage, and, as an armorer aboard the *Discovery*, had seen at Nootka Sound in 1778 what Cook alerted the western world to—the presence of innumerable sea otters. Chinese mandarins were already buying luxurious pelts at high prices from Russians exploiting the Aleutian Islands.

Dixon had decided to become a merchant-navigator, and the two-ship expedition of which he was part, financed by an English company, was the most ambitious to reach this coast since Cook's visit thirteen years earlier. Dixon put into a cove on Langara Island and soon found his ship surrounded by canoes full of people offering superb sea-otter pelts, many of which they had worn as cloaks. In less than half an hour, Dixon and his men acquired nearly 300 skins of excellent quality, and went on to pick up more, elated by their good fortune.

In the years that followed, many more traders of different nationalities came. Some of them were not as scrupulous in their dealings with the Haida as Dixon, who had made sure that every pelt was paid for. American traders came to be thoroughly detested. As late as 1878, the Canadian scientist George Dawson, upon meeting a Haida shaman fishing in a lonely spot, was asked whether he was a Boston man or a King George man. On being assured that Dawson and his party were not Americans, the old man commented, "Very good."

Sea otters were especially abundant in the waters frequented by

Sketch of Haida Indians in canoe, done at Port Rose Harbor, in 1793.

The Sea pale Indigo over pencil waves, is best

/ East Side /

Canoe with Indians at Port Rose, Queen Charlotte's Islands

Hatria's Wife

drawn after nature on friday 1 march 1793

Hatria a Chief in South End of Queen on the N.W. Coast of

Chief Hatria and his family at Port Rose Harbor, 1793.

the Haida and the Kaigani Haida, and hunting them preoccupied the people well into the 1800s, with one predictable result—a sharp decline in harvests. Fewer ships called. But, apart from the introduction of liquor and firearms, Haida life had not been greatly altered.

However, by the 1830s-1840s, the white man came closer by sea *and* land. The sea otter-oriented deep-sea traffic was replaced by coastal trading for pelts of land mammals—beaver, marten, land otter, bear. The Hudson's Bay Company (HBC) started a maritime trade on the coast, building strategically-located posts at which the furs could be collected from native hunters and put aboard its supply ships. Fur-trading posts were not entirely new to the Haida; they had visited the Russian one at Sitka since early in the century. Of the new posts, the first and most important because of its proximity was Fort Simpson, first established in 1831 and then moved to a better location in 1834. The Haida travelled to the post by canoe, both to trade with the HBC and to carry on their traditional trading with the Tsimshian and other mainlanders.

Gradually, as government evolved in British Columbia, the Haida began to lose their traditional freedoms, including those of raiding and slave-taking. Victoria, which had started out as a trading post in 1843 and grown into a colonial administrative center, exercised increasing control. Royal Navy gunboats were sent north as a "presence" and their masters remonstrated with the chiefs whenever incidents arose. The Haida harassed early mining expeditions to the Charlottes, apparently regarding these as forays onto their land. Similarly, they had a habit, distressing to whites, of claiming as theirs by right every movable object from American trading vessels wrecked in their waters, and ransoming crewmembers to the HBC, which then had difficulty obtaining recompense from the ship owners. To influential whites like the Royal Navy's James Prevost, the long-term solution seemed to be to induce missionaries to teach in the region. By the 1860s, Protestant missionaries had begun work permanently on the north coast. Church and state together imposed their strict ideas of law and order, the Protestant work ethic, and democratic ideals, none of which squared with the native way of life.

Meanwhile, city lights beckoned the younger generation. In 1858, when Victoria expanded from fewer than 300 whites to 6,000 following discovery of gold on the mainland, the Haida and other northern natives descended in the hundreds. They had come before

28

New totem at Haida village on Queen Charlotte Islands.

but never in such numbers. A worried Governor James Douglas had written in 1856: "I have used every means in my power to prevent their annual visits to white settlements, both British and American." Douglas, whose wife was part native, knew from long experience the potential harm of mass mixing of native people and white riff-raff, in this case rough miners from California, liquor peddlers, and the assorted hucksters who move into any boom town. In the Charlottes, older Haida regretted the depopulation of their villages.

Disease and alcohol-related deaths had already begun to take a serious toll. But in 1862 came the worst single disaster. A smallpox epidemic swept the native encampments at Victoria, and when the northerners were ordered away, they carried the disease along their escape routes. Soon whole communities lay dead and dying. Villages in the Charlottes suffered severely, especially those on the west coast. A chief summed up the feeling of utter despair: "Now the fires have gone out and the brave men have fallen before the iron man's sickness." Even many years afterwards, visitors to the villages that survived commented on the lack of children.

Smallpox wasn't the only disease. Influenza, measles, whooping cough, scarlet fever, tuberculosis, venereal disease, all killed or debilitated. By the end of the century, the survivors had been banded into the two villages of today, Skidegate and Old Masset.

The fatal impact left more than villages in ruins. A culture was in total disarray. As whites settled on the north coast, the new cash economy that replaced the old bartering system often kept poorer natives in perpetual debt to whites. In the same period, the authority of chiefs was undermined, and shamanism ridiculed into extinction. Potlatches, essential social events, were banned; carved poles, the great symbols of Haida inheritance and prestige, were destroyed; and Haida songs, dances and story-telling were silenced. For as long as the church influenced education, which was well into this century, promising children were removed from their home environment and sent to residential schools on the mainland, where the girls would be taught how to become servants in the homes of well-to-do whites and the boys how to be millworkers.

Only in the last thirty years has a new spirit of independence emerged among the Haida at home. Several factors have contributed to this. Better economic times have helped. More than a few Haida fishermen and loggers can call themselves well-off. They live in comfortable, modern houses; have television sets and well-stocked freezers; and vacation in Hawaii. Beyond this, though, the Haida have learned that their pride in their culture was well founded. The human rights movement, a greater understanding of the nature of power and how it works, with a resultant lessening of control by whites, and world-wide recognition of Haida arts have all gone far in restoring self-respect. Children now attend public schools in the Charlottes, and at Masset there is a class in the Haida language. Whereas the much-loved Methodist-United Church minister Peter Kelly was once the lone Haida of his calling, young Haida have entered this and other professions. Those of social conscience feel an obligation to help their people, whether in land claims or in combating the great waster of time and talent everywhere, alcoholism. From the memories of the old folks, thoughtful Haida retrieve as much as they can of the Haida past. And the talented ones are giving renewed expression to a brilliant artistic heritage.

Shells in a midden on the Queen Charlotte Islands.

LIVING OFF SEA AND LAND

Assuming that up to 10,000 Haida at one time inhabited the Charlottes, an island chain just over three hundred kilometers long and a hundred kilometers at greatest breadth, they were incredibly rich in resources per capita. They lived in the midst of a seafood pool that has since helped to feed the world. They were surrounded by magnificent forests from which they hewed timbers for housing and transportation (those famous canoes), and for highly functional articles of everyday equipment.

The sea was their principal source of food. Villages were always located within reach of productive halibut banks and salmon-spawning streams. Cleverly-designed harpoons, spears and fish-hooks of bone, horn or wood were used for single catches. Fishing lines were fashioned out of tightly-plaited natural fibers. In small streams, salmon were usually caught by weirs of split sticks, cylindrical baskets or flat frames. Halibut and salmon were relished fresh or dried. The women cleaned and filleted the fish, and preserved them by hanging them on wooden frames to dry. Once the sun or the slow fires beneath the frames had dried the catch, it was stored in cedar boxes.

Other fish such as trout, herring, flounder, ling cod, pollock, black cod, and rock cod were taken in abundance. Herring spawn was collected on kelp and again dried and stored away. Shellfish were handy at all times, and chitons and sea urchins were eaten in tremendous quantities.

For the necessary fat content of the diet, the Haida turned not so much to whaling, as did peoples of the west coast of Vancouver Island, but instead caught seals, rendered fish oil, and traded with the Tsimshian for the product of a fish they didn't have, the oolachan. Called *taow* and prized to this day, oolachan grease was eaten with all kinds of food.

As well as abundant seafoods, the Haida feasted on bear roasts, geese and ducks, birds' eggs, dried seaweed, ground roots and barks, salal berries, salmonberries, and wild crab apples. Nature spread a laden table.

From forests and marshes the Haida also obtained raw materials for making herbal medicines. Here much of the folklore has been lost, but we can assume that their detailed knowledge of what grew on their islands enabled them to accumulate a broad

pharmacology through the generations. Powder of the common puffball, to give one instance, was used for treating running sores and chapped hands. Roots and leaves of other plants were brewed for specific medicinal purposes.

The Haida were not plant propagators, with one notable exception. They cultivated a native tobacco plant for their own use and for trade. The cured leaves are believed to have been chewed primarily, but little is known about the plant or its narcotic properties as it has vanished in comparatively recent times. The Haida also cultivated extensive potato patches after the introduction of the tuber, probably by an early sea captain, and they traded their potatoes across to the mainland.

Fish Hooks and Harpoons

Spear Point

Fish drying on beach at Skidegate.

Halibut Hook

35

Ancestral Tools and Weapons

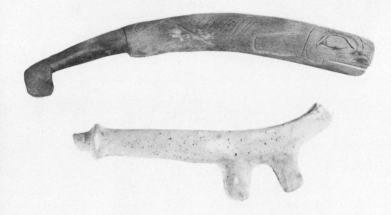

Fishing club.

"Slave killers," or ceremonial axes.

Club with perforation for wrist strap.

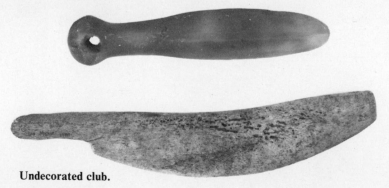

Undecorated club.

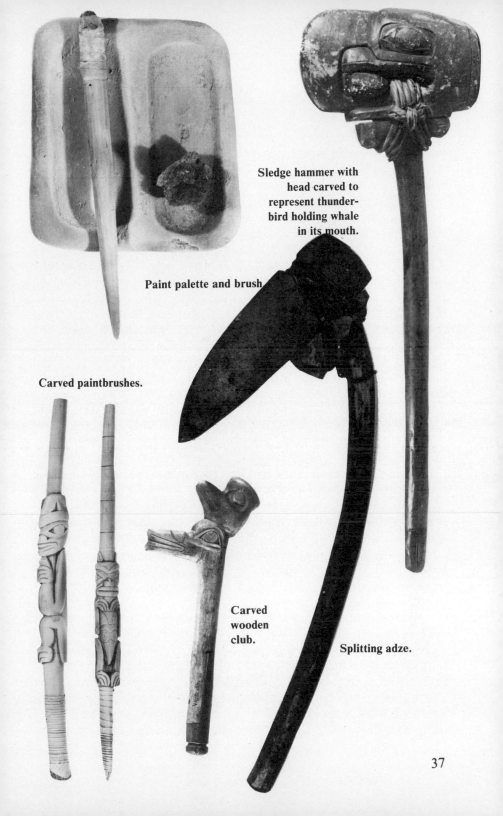

Paint palette and brush.

Sledge hammer with head carved to represent thunderbird holding whale in its mouth.

Carved paintbrushes.

Carved wooden club.

Splitting adze.

Working in Wood

Originally, the day-to-day life of the Haida revolved around their skillful use of wood, especially the western (red) cedar. Their works in cedar ranged from the massive to the minute, and their mastery of a technology based on wood was recognized from the very early days of European exploration.

Haida housing, rather more substantial than that of most other coastal people, used large cedar posts and split planks. These were family houses, square or designed as long houses up to fifteen meters long and twelve meters wide. They accommodated maybe fifteen people, and were arranged in rows at the permanent villages, either side by side or slightly separated. A person wishing to build a house had first to accumulate sufficient property. Parties of thirty to forty men went by canoe, singing, to the cedar stand, where the chiefs directed operations. The trees for uprights and beams were trimmed whole, and planks were hewn on the spot. Then all the materials for the house were towed to the village. The crafting was done with wooden wedges, stone hammers, and hafted axes and adzes of polished basalt and nephrite. The split planks, dressed on both sides with knives of California mussel and further scraped with shell, were so smooth as to appear sawn. Inside the gabled house, the ground area was either flat or stepped-down to a central fireplace. An opening in the pitched roof admitted light and at the same time emitted smoke from the hearth.

Arranged around were the household belongings—food, clothing, implements, usually stored in boxes of cedar. The box sides were made from a single, thin, wide piece of cedar bent three times at a right angle and joined with wooden pegs. Cedar slabs formed the bases and lids. Light to carry, yet strong, these boxes were so well made as to be watertight. Taken on canoe trips, they bore trade goods back and forth.

Haida canoes, made of hollowed-out cedar trees, gave their makers an envied reputation. In size, they ranged from small dugouts, designed for one or two persons, to vessels fifteen meters long, with sleek lines and clipper-like prows, capable of carrying forty people and two-ton cargoes. Even the largest canoes were fast and amazingly seaworthy, though now and then, despite adroit handling, full canoes were caught in stormy seas and their occupants drowned. The logs were rough-shaped where the tree was

Bentwood storage box.

Massett Village

Feast Bowl

cut, then finished off in the village with more hollowing, steaming with water and hot stones, insertion of thwarts to give the required beam, and carving of the prow. The Haida traded their canoes, and took great care of their own to prevent them from drying out. Canoe-making virtually ceased after the introduction of gasoline-powered boats around 1910.

The other great works in cedar were much less utilitarian but tremendously important in the Haida system of values. These were the carved columns: interior house posts; exterior house frontal poles; and, also outdoors and free-standing, memorial poles and shorter mortuary posts. All were carved with crest figures symbolic of lineage, status, and significant events. Large grave figures were also carved out of red cedar. The memorial poles and frontal poles could reach eighteen meters in height and one and a half meters in width. Frontal poles placed at the center front of houses often had oval doorways cut through their bases. Pole carvers were highly-regarded artisans, and pole raisings, like house raisings, were occasions for ceremony. The cedar of houses and poles bleached light gray under the weather, contrasting sharply with the deep green of the surrounding forests. This green has now completely enclosed the long-deserted villages.

As well as the monumental works in red cedar, we must admire also the smaller creations in red cedar and other woods such as yellow cedar, alder, yew, maple, spruce, crab apple—the practical items such as bent boxes, bowls and platters, paddles and canoe balers, fish clubs and fish hooks; the ceremonial articles such as masks, rattles, and whistles; the personal adornments such as cloak fasteners, charms, and labrets (lip plugs); and the goods made of wood fibers such as mats, baskets, and hats. We admire them not only because each served its purpose very well, but also because most of them were decorated with Haida designs, or sometimes actually given the three-dimensional shape of a Haida crest figure (a frog bowl or a cormorant rattle, for example). The objective was crest and/or story portrayal showing the owner's right to use these symbols of design, to show rank, status, and lineage affiliation, and it summoned up amazing artistic ingenuity.

For a long time, the cultural integrity of these creations eluded outsiders. But the obvious combination of the functional and the beautiful made Haida artifacts much sought by museums and private collectors. Just as the first white traders had bought the very clothing that Haida people wore, those cloaks of lustrous sea otter fur, so, later, the Haida were virtually stripped of their other belongings. The fact that many Haida willingly sold or generously gave away their possessions does not deny the loss. It deprived two generations of a chance to see what their predecessors had created. Between 1900 and 1950, young, potential artists hadn't the money to travel to study the expatriated works. However, in the fifty-year period, tenacious Haida carvers and silver engravers continued to produce works illustrative (if not firmly in the context) of their culture, and youngsters watched and learned from them. Equally important, other British Columbians, especially north coast residents, bought. The presentation of Haida and Tsimshian carvings as going-away gifts is traditional in Prince Rupert. In fact, the supporting role of whites in the Charlottes and Prince Rupert has been greatly underestimated. Outsiders have little idea of the rapport that has long existed between long-time white residents and native peoples on the north coast. Both groups have had to make their way on their own, largely ignored and at times even hindered by the white population-power centers in the south of the province, and as a result they have given each other a great deal of moral support. At all levels the two peoples tend to mingle more than whites and natives in the south.

Now, gradually, Haida art is coming home. It arrived first in photographs published in readily-available books. Then came government-sponsored grants enabling young Haida to travel and study. And in that fine, modern institution, the Queen Charlotte Islands Museum at Skidegate, the Haida can now see their works on loan and permanent exhibition.

Housing

Drawing of Haida house showing locations of poles.

Skedans houses stand shoulder to shoulder like townhouses.
National Museum of Canada, Ottawa

Interior of Chief Weah's house, Masset, 1884-1888.

A band of Haida erecting a house at the Tsimshian village of Port Simpson, 1866.

Canoes

**Felled tree, roughly cut
into shape of canoe.**

Removing the covers after steaming, Masset. National Museum of Canada, Ottawa   Neg. #2666

Fitting a piece onto a canoe bow, Masset.

Canoes on the beach at Skidegate, 1878.

Totems

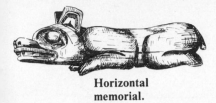

Horizontal
memorial.

House
frontal.

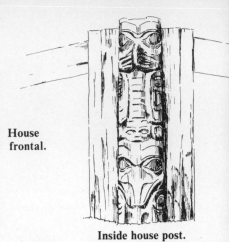

Inside house post.

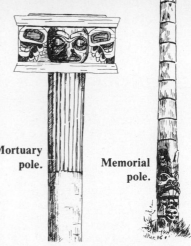

Mortuary
pole.

Memorial
pole.

Head of a spirit figure.

Totems fronting houses at Skidegate. Photo: G.M. Dawson, 1878.

Poles at Massett now in Berlin Museum.

Haida country, an incongruous blend of calm bays and lagoons, sandy beaches and rocky tide pools, boggy meadows and snowy mountains, gigantic forests and stunted scrubland.

Blue grouse.

Pacific Mune—eggs and
birds were valued foods.

otter hunt.
nting by Lars Belmonte.

Sea lions.

Ninstints Village, Anthony Island. →

Double-columned mortuary pole, Skedans.

Silent watcher leans away from the p

Hat weaver. Painting by Susan Imbaugarten.

Agnes Russ. Painted by Mildred Valley Thornt◄

Haida pole carver. Painting by Mildred Valley Thornton.

Ed Caesar working pole.

Claude Davidson raven and eagle house front design, painted by Jim Hart. Carved door shows weeping bear design.

Rufus Moody of Skidegate.

Magnificent old Haida

Plaited inner cedar bark basket.
Lightbawn collection.

Twined spruce root storage basket.
L. Lightbawn collection.

Spruce root twined trinket baskets.
Queen Charlotte Island Museum collection

Twining a fine spruce root hat.
by Primrose Adams

Gold brooch by Bill Reid.
Anne Sinclaire collection

**Modern stylized Haida painting
by Pat McGuire**

Reg Ashwell Collection

House pole at Tanu. Photo: C.F. Newcombe, 1903
B.C. Provincial Museum, Victoria

Haida meeting house, Haida.

Monuments

Totem pole near Tow Hill, Graham Island, 1919.

Department of Mines Geological Survey
Neg. #46694

Detail of pole, showing carved frog.

Detail of pole at Ninstints.

Containers

Painted box.

National Museum of Canada, Ottawa
Neg. #J 18713-4

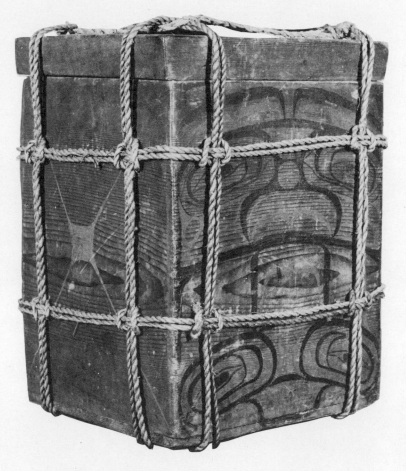

An assortment of carved wooden containers.

Masks

Haida masks.

Haida masks.

Symbolic Decoration

Artistic expression is the great characteristic of northwest coast native peoples. Artwork in stone, the most durable material, has been dated back thousands of years—in the Queen Charlotte Islands 4,000 years—and archaeology has barely scratched the surface. In the records of the first white traders, who were mainly interested in gathering up furs and getting away fast with their ships intact, Haida artistic achievements were scarcely mentioned. Educated men of the 1791 French scientific expedition of Etienne Marchand, however, looked more closely than the average trader. They saw huge carvings, painted boards, even panpipes, and commented that here "architecture, sculpture, painting, and music are found united."

How united they were, and the degree to which they were integrated into the culture, wasn't realized until much later, when the designs were understood, but the impression that struck the Frenchmen, of "paintings everywhere, everywhere sculpture," gives us some idea of the ubiquity of Haida art in the villages of the late eighteenth century. The Haida painted and carved designs on wooden structures and a bewildering array of household and ceremonial articles. The decorative arts were apparent in their villages, their homes, their dress. The use of designs to show the owner's status and lineage affiliation was of prime importance. We have no way of knowing the range of crest designs painted on wood in the eighteenth century and the early nineteenth century, but early argillite carvings, notably the panel pipes of Haida motif, suggest a greater variety of representations, indeed a richer ceremonial imagery, than appeared later. Quite probably there were local and regional design differences as well.

From the ethnological record, we do know that the shape of many objects for household and ceremonial use (boxes, bowls, rattles, for example) changed not at all as white influence pervaded the culture, having stood the test of a very long time, but that certain objects were no longer made (war helmets are one example, labrets another) and that others changed extraordinarily.

Everyone wears Western apparel today, but Haida clothing used to be very distinctive. The first accounts tell of men and women wearing fur or cedar-bark cloaks over tunics of tanned skins. The women's tunics ranged in length from below the knee to the ankle,

Front and back view of a ceremonial shirt.

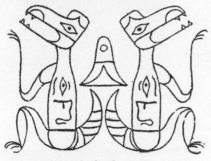 

Tattoo from the back of Chief Kitkun, of *Wasco*, the wolf-fish.

Tattoo from the back of a Haida Indian, of the thunderbird.

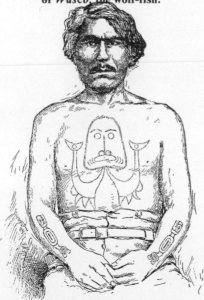 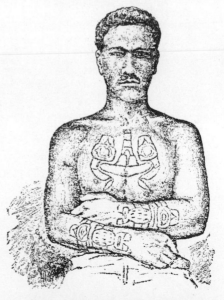

Tattoos on Chief Kitkun. On his chest is *Kahatla*, the cod, and on his arms is *Cheena*, the salmon.

Young Haida with tattoos. On his chest is *Hoorts*, the bear, and on each of his forearms is *Koot*, the eagle.

"Totem" Poles at Massett, Q.C.I.

and were made of deerskin or caribou hides traded from the mainland. The garments were often trimmed with ornaments such as puffin beaks. In ceremonial outfits, including headdresses, there was probably great variety. In the 1800s, the Haida adopted Western dress—coats and trousers, shawls and skirts. However, the cloak found a successor when the Hudson's Bay trade blanket came along around the middle of the century. It was made desirable by the fact that it was used as currency and therefore had prestige value. The heavy navy blue blanket later took on ceremonial status when worn as a cloak emblazoned with red flannel borders and crest designs trimmed with dentalium shell or mother-of-pearl buttons. Today, Haida button blankets are usually made of black woolen cloth with red woolen cloth borders on the top and sides. The principal crest of the wearer is appliqued on the blanket face in the same red material. The buttons are made of ivory-like plastic. Owners of button blankets wear them on ceremonial occasions, and dancers performing in these brilliant cloaks present a colorful spectacle.

Eminent Haida chiefs and shamans at one time wore beautiful Chilkat cloaks—actually blankets woven in intricate designs from mountain-goat wool and traded by northern mainlanders for Haida canoes. The best-known ceremonial headdresses of Haida chiefs were of the frontlet type common also to the Tsimshian and Tlingit. A major crest figure was handsomely carved and inlaid in the form of a wooden panel worn above the forehead. Surmounting the panel was a circle of sea-lion bristles "fencing" a hollow crown containing down which could be shaken out by the wearer onto others as a sign of goodwill. A deep fringe of ermine pelts framed the headdress. With adaptations, the making of these is being revived for initiations of hereditary chiefs.

Personal decoration went all the way from face paint and body tattoos to hairpieces, facial adornments, neck pieces, bracelets, and ankle rings. They also used treated mineral, charcoal and ochre paints, cedar bark, bone, feathers, shells, horn, metal—in fact, almost anything that could carry designs effectively. The silver and gold bracelets of Haida women are reflections today. These finely-engraved bracelets are made for them or have been handed down in the family, and several may be worn on the arm at one time. Haida craftsmen excelled at making bracelets in silver and gold, and maintain the reputation today.

THE RICHER MEANING OF LIFE

Ravens and Eagles

Like other native peoples of the northwest coast, the Haida had a rich, complex social system based on kinship and rank. Many facets of this system have been greatly altered or lost entirely and, as the anthropologist Wilson Duff once wrote, in this aspect of culture, perhaps more than in others, the Indians have given up more than they received in return. However, some facets of the Haida social system remain pertinent today, and to begin to understand Haida art forms we must know something of that structure.

Every Haida is by birth either a Raven or an Eagle. Ravens and Eagles are the two exogamous divisions. Affiliation with either moiety is hereditary, determined by one's mother's affiliation. Thus, every Haida belongs by birth to the moiety of his or her mother. Within the moieties are lineages and more localized social groupings, and with them are associated a great many names, crests, legends, and songs. These are usually passed on to a nephew according to the rules of matrilineal inheritance—that is, through a man's eldest sister to her eldest son. All are property, like chieftainships, ownership of houses, or rights to certain fishing grounds.

Whether one is an Eagle or a Raven is taken for granted; this is known by everyone who knows the mother's line. A person's principal crest or crests, on the other hand, are what he uses and prizes for personal identity, ceremonials, and displays: killer whale, for example, oldest crest of the Ravens, or beaver, used by many Eagle families. These symbols of background are bestowed within a family, earned by a person in his lifetime, or inherited or acquired by adoption. Raven crests are, on the whole, distinct from Eagle crests. Crests represent supernatural birds or animals, sometimes manifestations of nature such as rainbow, and occasionally man-made objects. Many go back far in legendry, to the exploits of founding figures and their heirs, back to a lineage ancestor who acquired supernatural powers through the bird or animal represented.

The ancestor of the Ravens is said to be Foam Woman, who rose from the sea; the Eagle moiety claims descent from Djilaqons, a contemporary of Foam Woman. Djilaqons eventually became a

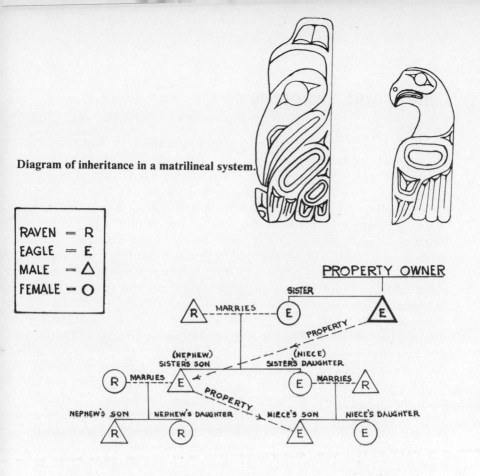

Diagram of inheritance in a matrilineal system.

RAVEN = R
EAGLE = E
MALE = △
FEMALE = ○

PROPERTY OWNER

SISTER

R — MARRIES — E

E

PROPERTY

(NEPHEW)
SISTERS SON

(NIECE)
SISTERS DAUGHTER

R — MARRIES — E

E — MARRIES — R

PROPERTY

NEPHEW'S SON

NEPHEW'S DAUGHTER

NIECE'S SON

NIECE'S DAUGHTER

R

R

E

E

mountain in the Ninstints region. Offspring of the founders in turn gave rise to groupings named after the places where they made their permanent homes, such as Those-born-at-Rose-Spit or Those-born-at-Koona. Outstanding men and women in each lineage provided, by their actions, the substance for stories, songs, and dances which families for generations told and retold, often with variations.

A Haida story told to C.F. Newcombe illustrates just one way in which a legend might be reiterated. In one of the stories relating to the destruction by fire of a story town on Cumshewa Inlet called Djigua, after the death of all the inhabitants but one, Djilaqons sang an especially-poignant song of mourning. This was one of ten songs used in ceremonies held in memory of Captain Kloo, the great Eagle chief of Skedans and Tanu, who drowned in 1903.

Chiefs and Shamans

In the old days the Haida had what amounted to a class system based on wealth and rank. Chiefs had rank in terms of position, and others had rank in terms of social status, formalized in each case by the potlatch. Few people had no status at all, as there was always upward mobility through adoption by rich relatives. Chiefs inherited their rank, and if they had high social status, so much the better. However, the chiefs themselves were by no means equal and this more than anything else often led to intense rivalry. There were chiefs of Eagle or Raven lineages with adherents living in one or more villages; there were town (village) chiefs and the chiefs of households. Each inherited his position usually, though not always, from an older brother or a maternal uncle, and to maintain or enhance that position he had to be generous in his displays of wealth and what he gave away at potlatches.

Like leaders everywhere, the chiefs had the highest profiles in their communities. The names of a good many have come down from the last century: Scotsgai, Nestacaana, Skidegate, Ninstints, Weah, Edenshaw, to mention only a few. Sometimes, as in the case of Ninstints or Skedans, a village would be called after a prominent chief of that village. Occasionally a woman became a chief. Under the system of matrilineal inheritance women could be power brokers. In the years of intense fur trading, it was often the women who decided whether a bargain would be struck and under what terms.

While a chief had powers over (and responsibilities to) his lineage, his village, or his household, none ruled absolutely. "He has no power of compelling work from other members of the tribe," George Dawson wrote. "Should he require a new house he must pay for its erection by making a distribution of property, just as any other man of the tribe would do; and indeed it is expected of the chief that he shall be particularly liberal in these givings away, as well as in providing feasts for the people." Chiefs could lead raids against other Haida chiefs and their kinsmen, and against mainland villages of the Tlingit, Tsimshian, and Kwakiutl. Slaves were obtained from the latter sources, and the number of these workers in a chief's household usually indicated his rank. Slave holdings seem not to have been large, at least in historical times.

Under pressure from the white authorities, slave-taking ceased

Shaman's rattle.

Shaman's grave box.

in the last century. The power of the chiefs, too, was greatly reduced after the 1880s when whites began settling in the Charlottes and starting private and commercial enterprises on lands to which the chiefs held rights by tradition. Chieftainships also lapsed, never to be restored.

Even so, in the 1960s, after two generations of Haida had been under direct control of the federal Indian Affairs department through a resident agent, and election of chiefs and councillors had been established, people in Skidegate still knew who their hereditary chiefs were. One had only to make casual inquiry, as this writer did, to compile the following list: Solomon Wilson, an Eagle lineage chief; Lewis Collinson, Chief Skidegate; George Young, Chief Skedans; Albert Jones, Chief Ninstints; Nathan Young, Chief Kloo;

Argillite carving of medicine man.

Charles Wesley, Chief Cumshewa. In their extensive families, these chiefs were respected for their knowledge of the Haida past, and some, like Solomon Wilson, willingly shared that knowledge with researchers. Albert Jones, by the way, was co-discoverer of the iron mine at Tasu.

The other prominent figures in early Haida life were the shamans, men or women recognized as having powers beyond those of ordinary mortals. A shaman served as an intermediary for supernatural beings, and could temporarily lose his own identity in the process. He was both doctor and clairvoyant endowed with special skills and sensitivity, and was consulted on all vital matters of life and death. Before taking a raiding party afield, a chief sought his advice on omens concerning the weather and chances of victory. The shaman's insight enabled him to interpret, through dreams or visions, into precisely which child the spirit of a dead person would return. And, by the use of an instrument called a soul-catcher, he could reputedly capture the departing spirit of a seriously-ill patient and with it restore full life.

Unfortunately, little is known about the shamans and their practices. Even to their fellow Haida they were shadowy figures who lived apart. In the last century, shamans were called *sGaga*, derived from a word meaning long-haired ones—shamans of both sexes wore their hair long, and tied in a knot on the crown of the head. Each *sGaga* and his one or two apprentices kept most of their arcane knowledge to themselves. If their secrets were disclosed to others, they stood to lose their powers, which seems reasonable enough: any secret revealed ceases to be a secret. Before the piercingly cool eye of modern science could be focused on the shamans, they had collided with the missionary and come out bitter losers. They lost partly on medical grounds, to vaccines and chemical pain-killers; yet when their profession died in the 1880s so also died any hope of retrieving the full range of their herbal, psychological, and artistic information.

A few photographs of Haida chiefs and of shamans, taken separately, survive from the last century, affirming written descriptions. For the best depictions, though, we need look no further than Haida argillite carvings, where we can actually see changes in costume styles; for example, some figurines show a cedar-bark rope of status worn like a sash. In this unique art, the Haida unconsciously recorded changes in their culture in a progression that has no equivalent in the arts of other northwest coast native peoples.

Customs and Ceremonials

When Haida life pulsed according to the seasons, the spring to autumn period was devoted to food gathering and food storing, and the late autumn and winter period to ceremonials, mainly potlatches and winter dances.

The potlatch, practiced by all coastal peoples, was basically a redistribution of wealth by someone to mark an important event—a move up in rank, a tattooing or some other stage of growing up, a house-building, a memorial commemoration, for instance—and it brought villagers together for days of feasting, dancing, gambling with sticks, and ritual observances. The unique feature was that some guests had an obligation to return later to the giver more than they received. White officialdom regarded potlatches as not only wasteful and heathenish but a hindrance to their imposition of church-going and schooling, and therefore banned them in 1884. For a time, Haida people defied the ban, and several elderly Haida today remember hearing of the heavy fines levied on their forefathers for holding illegal potlatches.

In hindsight, the potlatch seems positively ingenious. In a wealthy society like that of the Haida, it spread the riches and kept people busy creating more. Apart from economics, though, the potlatch maintained social cohesion and recurringly stimulated creativity in the arts. Everyone took part in the preparations, whether in a major or minor role, from chiefs to slaves. Anticipation of the next festival gave infinite zest to life.

Potlatches were by no means the only occasions for display and ceremony. The arrival of a Tsimshian group bringing oolachan grease would be worthy of celebration over several days. In the home villages, family groupings held ceremonies marking personal feats, initiations, name-givings, marriages, deaths. Secret societies had their rites also.

Whatever was being commemorated, the event was expressed in song, dance or oratory (perhaps all three), composed for the occasion or handed down through generations. The dancing involved the wearing of dance hats and costumes and, depending on the type of dance, masks, and the use of drums, rattles, and whistles. The songs, strong in rhythm and vocal line, were sung for specific purposes. There were songs of love, of mourning, of mating, of war, of peace-making, of welcome, rain songs, dreamer (prophet) songs,

**Wooden grease dish, carved in the shape of a wolf.
Collected by C.F. Newcombe, in 1912.**

Haida shamans at Masset.

Shaman's rattle.

Horned owl design on a copper.

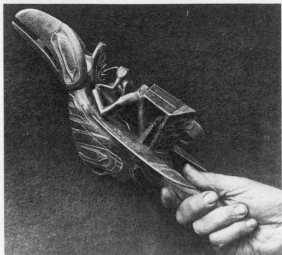

Copied from: *The North American Indian.* Volume 11 — opposite page 138. 1915.

and on and on. When women went into the forests to gather spruce roots for basket-making, they sang a song associated with that activity. In a sense, work was not work as we know it but yet another ceremony.

This formal, ceremonial aspect to all of life's endeavors was closely related to the Haida perception of an ordered (if sometimes unpredictable) world around him. He considered himself very much a part of nature. He lived in harmony with the many birds and animal species of his immediate environment and therefore felt one with them. Animals could be defined in human terms and vice versa. The relationship was old and deeply symbiotic.

All living things were imbued with supernatural powers. Every animal was, or might be, the embodiment of a being who could appear in a human form of his own free will. This did not mean that they could not be hunted, or presented as food to the Haida by another animal who was also a supernatural being. Furthermore, the supernaturals had a community life of their own. They could take human beings into their villages, mate with them, and help or harm them, just as man would do with other members of his own species. Raven was a prime example of interchangeability, capable

84

of taking different visible forms, transforming things, and playing tricks. Because of the uncertainty of his role at any given moment, he had to be treated with respect.

There were other creatures of legend, some closely linked with certain villages, moieties and lineages, and taken as crests. Wasco was one. To some Haida he was sea wolf, to others grizzly bear of the sea, and yet others, sea dog. Wasco was a hunter of whales, and he had ties with Skidegate, since he reputedly lived in a mountain lake behind the village.

Wasco and the other personae of legend were very real. Many had specific attributes and origins. A young woman could be seduced by a bear and give birth to a child that was sometimes human and sometimes bear. She thus became the bear-mother of legend. Under certain circumstances, a girl could be transformed into a sea creature, and changed back again later. To be alert to the possibilities of a situation, one had to know the legends. Always one had to be conscious of the possibility of the double take. An old man working on a canoe at the other end of the village might be heron in disguise, guarding a killer whale village that lay beneath the sea. Cedar bark, to some Haida, was every woman's elder sister.

There existed—and still does exist—a concept of rebirth. A person could be reborn several times, embodied in others. The transfer of identity was often made to a new-born relative. "I am my grandfather," a young man will say today. The act of transfer took place when he was born. Another Haida will say she is the reincarnation of her grandfather's sister who died in childhood. It was a symbolic, unifying gesture that reinforced pride in individual heritage.

The Haida gave themselves (and their family houses) descriptive names. In the naming of individuals, several different names were given, each marking a step toward adulthood, and the choice was often the name of a relative who had died. These personal names descended through the mother's line, and when the missionaries baptised Haida converts and gave them Anglo-Saxon first names and surnames (often of prominent white people) which are passed down in the paternal line, they skewed another Haida tradition. Today, Haida names continue to be bestowed matrilineally, both to family members and to those accepted into the family by adoption. Many Haida artists use both their Canadian and their Haida names—for example, Ed Russ (Gitajung), Thomas Hans (Iyea), Lavina Lightbown (Ta-how-hegelths).

ARTS OF THE HAIDA
Life and Art and Learning

Where art forms were so much a part of the culture, tightly woven as its very fabric, we must look at what happened to the most familiar arts of the Haida during more than one hundred years of sweeping change. The enforced end to major ceremonial gatherings suppressed singing, dancing, and oratory, as well as the crafting of artifacts associated with those performing arts, such as masks, rattles and speakers' staffs. (The demise of shamanism further undermined Haida crafts, dooming the making of masks, rattles, and other devices pertaining to the shaman's office.) Songs and dances faded in the memory as Haida performers were turned into hymn singers and brass band musicians. The creative spirit could no longer function as it once did. Many songs composed in the 1800s, some of which commemorated episodes involving white people, survive only in snatches.

Even so, a few elderly Haida know the words and movements of family song and dance performances, and teach them to younger Haida people wishing to form entertainment groups. Masset people, especially members of the old, proud families like the Edenshaws, have come to the fore in organizing Haida dancing. Songs have been recorded since the early 1950s and may in the future inspire revivals.

Storytelling, though much more limited than it was in the old days of ceremonial gatherings, goes on in the homes. Grandparents and uncles and aunts pass on family legends to the children informally, with memory training. "Listen closely, I will tell you this story only once," an elder exhorted. That was the old Haida way, and may be the reason why the Haida are, on the whole, good listeners. Capability in speech-making seems to have lost little over the years. A person like the late William Matthews, Masset's Chief Weah, in old age could hold audiences spellbound one minute and have them in fits of laughter the next. Talented individuals use the Haida language to profound effect on public occasions.

But what the world sees of Haida arts are the sculptural and graphic forms, and here the traditions in design are formal and awesomely disciplined. Once we go beyond technical details, words fail: design is its own language. However, two-dimensional Haida

Old Haida totem.

design has basic elements common to that of other northwest coast peoples—similar form lines and spatial organization—and many early two-dimensional Haida designs are very difficult to distinguish from Tsimshian and Tlingit examples when they depict the same crests. In sculptural art, on the other hand, Haida characteristics become more apparent. In the crests on carved poles we see a "fullness" in the shape of the Haida eye, in the broad brows that are subtler than the thinner, arched brows of Tlingit and Tsimshian art, and even in the limbs; and almost equal proportioning of face to body. If we can talk of a classic style in Haida poles, the best illustration is a pole standing outside the main entrance to the Provincial Museum in Victoria. In every aspect, it is pure Haida. Generally speaking, the Haida regard their designs as less "busily" elaborated than those of the Tlingit, and more abstract than Tsimshian designs. Anatomical features of crests in Haida graphic art are sometimes organized as total abstracts.

Carved poles and posts left in the deserted villages were avidly sought by outsiders for display in cities around the world. The collector C.F. Newcombe, from 1895 to his death in 1924, bought at least fifty poles and posts from their Haida owners and had them shipped as far away as Australia. Several poles were also removed to Prince Rupert. In the last major removal, in 1957, the Provincial Museum and the University of British Columbia with the permission of the Skidegate band council took sixteen sections of eleven poles and posts from Ninstints for safekeeping and study at Victoria and Vancouver. Ninstints, never designated as an Indian reserve, then had the largest number intact—about thirty-five. After all the removals, legal and illegal, only poles too fragile for anyone to handle were left behind. The only stands of old poles easily accessible in the north coast region of British Columbia are those of the Gitksan Tsimshian villages on and near the upper Skeena River.

Haida capability in producing massive works in cedar is still being demonstrated, though much less frequently than it was in the last century, up to about 1880. In 1969, Robert Davidson, anxious to restore traditions in his home village of Old Masset, carved a twelve-meter-high pole which was erected with ceremony. For its community long house, Skidegate has a house-frontal pole carved over a nine-month period by Bill Reid, assisted by Gary Edenshaw. This pole is the new companion for a weather-beaten pole that somehow survived the mass destruction of poles at Skidegate and Old Masset.

Anthony Island totem pole expedition, 1957.

Artistic talent today focuses on woodcarvings small and large, silver and gold jewelry, argillite carving, prints, and a limited amount of hand-weaving. The artists learn from each other, studying works of previous artists and examining the techniques of their contemporaries. As they gain competence, they develop their own styles. Mastery of design basics is essential. Consequently, a number of artists are highly skilled in more than one medium, as were most of the outstanding artists of the past, most notably Charles Edenshaw.

Charles Edenshaw and His Successors

Charles Edenshaw, who lived from about 1850 to 1920, did more than anyone else to establish Haida craftsmanship as art in the eyes of the international community. By his own example, he compelled the outside world to acknowledge all Haida artists. His output was immense, versatile, consistently of high quality.

Skidegate-born, Edenshaw is said to have grown up in the household of his uncle, Albert Edward Edenshaw (1810?-1894), a leading chief of the Stastas Eagles of Kiusta, one of the Eagle moiety groupings. Albert Edward was noted as an ironworker, coppersmith, jewelry maker, and carver of poles, and from him Charles learned the basics of designing, carving, and painting. From his mother and her eminent brother, whom he succeeded as Chief Edenshaw, Charles acquired specific crests and legends of the Stastas Eagles lineage. The surname was an anglicized version of the old family name *Edinso* or *It-in-su*.

To the quiet, dignified Edenshaw, chieftainship meant responsibility more than rights and prestige. He looked after the well-being of members of his lineage throughout the islands, raised his own family, spared time for the questions of visiting scientists and government officials, helped build the Anglican church at Masset, and all the while produced first-class art.

In that art, design was all-important. He had abundant crests and legends to be translated into designs, and the technical ability to render them in various mediums, often with unprecedented embellishments. In wood, he produced a great many carvings large and small, including poles. He painted designs on houses, on canoes, on woven hats, and on baskets. He carved ivory handles for walking sticks. He made jewelry. He carved prodigiously in argillite.

Yet there are two related paradoxes to Edenshaw's life and work. One is that while he was well known in his lifetime, the recognition he deserved did not come until years after his death, when northwest coast native art was hailed internationally by European interpreters around the time of World War II. Ultimately, Edenshaw was acknowledged as one of Canada's foremost artists. The other paradox is that, although he produced a vast number of works, precious few are known definitely as being from his hand. Most of the Edenshaws in museums are attributions—expert opinions based on style characteristics. Edenshaw didn't sign his

One of the few
photographs of
Charles Edenshaw
carving, taken about
1906.
Provincial Archives,
Victoria, B.C.

pieces; nor did others of his own and previous generations. In their eyes, art spoke for itself.

For the last thirty years, the acclaimed master of Haida art has been Bill Reid of Vancouver, born in 1920 and of Haida descent through his mother. His maternal grandfather, Charles Gladstone, a silversmith and argillite and wood carver of Skidegate, and a relative of Charles Edenshaw, is one of the bridging figures in twentieth century Haida art. Reid, a quiet, thoughtful man, has created one masterwork after another, each exciting in concept and exquisite in detail. His guiding principle of innovation within tradition has been applied with enormous success to the major art forms, jewelry-making especially, and his work commands the highest prices of any northwest coast native artist.

Reid reached the top by constant study and hard work. His first career was in radio; he was a CBC announcer in Vancouver and Toronto. But a growing interest in jewelry-making and Haida design gradually took him into a very different career where he would gain pre-eminence. He trained and apprenticed in European jewelry techniques in Toronto, and, after returning to Vancouver in

The ivory handle and silver band of a walking stick made by Charles Edenshaw, with raven design on band. Formerly in the Jelliman collection, museum #10677.

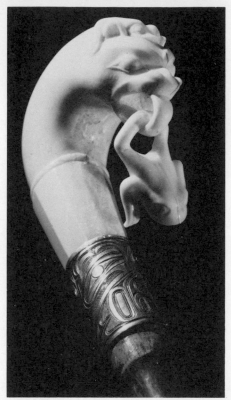

Detail of argillite carving showing beaver with Raven's son in center of tail. Note bear cub between ears and raven's tail.

National Museum of Canada, Ottawa

Silver bracelet attributed to Charles Edenshaw. Split eagle design.

Ethnology Division
B.C. Provincial Museum, Victoria
Neg. #10677

1951 and privately studying and reproducing Edenshaw designs, began putting what he had learned into practice. In Vancouver in the 1950s, Reid was in the right place at the right time. Private collectors began buying his work, and commissions came his way. From 1958 to 1962 he was engaged in a Haida wood-carving project at the University of British Columbia. In 1967, at the Arts of the Raven exhibition mounted by the Vancouver Art Gallery, Reid jewelry and argillite carvings stood out among contemporary works, and at his first one-man show, a retrospective at the same gallery in 1974, the full glory of Reid's work opened to public view. It encompassed some of his most productive years and, by his own assessment, the three best years when he worked in Montreal in Haida and contemporary design. In his gold boxes, superbly crafted, Reid introduced repoussé, chasing, and lost wax casting techniques, which other Haida jewelry makers have adopted. By going further into the world, Reid added a dimension to Haida art, expanding its prospects.

Reid's protégé, Robert Davidson, a great-grandson of Charles Edenshaw, is both a conventional and an innovative designer whose creations are much in demand in a widening market. Born in Hydaburg in 1946, Davidson grew up in Old Masset and, in the traditional manner, learned carving by watching older family members at work, particularly his grandfather, Robert Davidson Sr. The young Davidson moved to Vancouver in 1965 and there learned pole-carving and silversmithing from Bill Reid, attended art courses, created major works in cedar, and later moved into the then-developing field of printmaking, where he designed prolifically and actually made his own prints. His one-man show at the Vancouver Centennial Museum in 1971 was the first for a northwest coast native artist. Davidson exemplifies his family's creative vitality. The Edenshaw-Davidson lines, which have strong Kaigani links, have many members who have been signally astute in encouraging Haida art and giving it continuity.

The wellspring of Haida art flows back at home, in the Charlottes, and here many artists of distinction have labored through the years without benefit of publicity. One thinks of the designer, jewelry maker and argillite carver Tom Price, the goldsmith Art Adams, the argillite carver Pat McGuire, and the multi-talented Yeltatzie family, to recall only a very few. People like them have helped give the Haida the reputation that Wilson Duff once ascribed to them, the most intensely artistic of the northwest coast.

Major Components

· The arts that survived did so because Haida artists wanted to display their designs portraying their crests and legends—and because enough outsiders wanted their creations. Where the raw materials have been available and markets have opened up, the Haida artist has been ready to seize an opportunity.

In the old culture, many articles were made not only for Haida use but also for gifts and trade to other native peoples. Even then, not all items for home use were abundant. For example, nettle nets used with fish traps were very valuable because they took a long time to make (only chiefs with fish trap sites possessed these nets), and mats made of cattail stems were prized for the same reason. Masterworks in ceremonial regalia were given or traded outside if the occasion warranted, and with them were bestowed the songs and stories associated with those belongings.

In the extension of this trade into the modern marketplace, availability of the raw material was a key factor. Consider two of the items made for home use and trade in the 1800s—bracelets and horn spoons. Bracelet-making advanced first when silver currency came into circulation on the north coast and has continued with the availability of precious metal. The making of elegant horn spoons and ladles with elaborately-carved handles, a specialty of the Tlingit but also produced by the Haida, might have continued had not the raw material become scarce. The mountain sheep and mountain goat horns previously traded by interior native peoples to the Tlingit and Tsimshian, and then on to the Haida because neither animal existed on the Charlottes, could no longer be procured easily or cheaply enough to justify the difficult work of spoon-making.

It is often impossible to draw a dividing line between what was made for home use, what was made for gifts, and what was made for trade in Western terms of retail sale. For a long time they overlapped, especially in ceremonial articles.

These are the major fields of creativity today:

Medicine rattles.

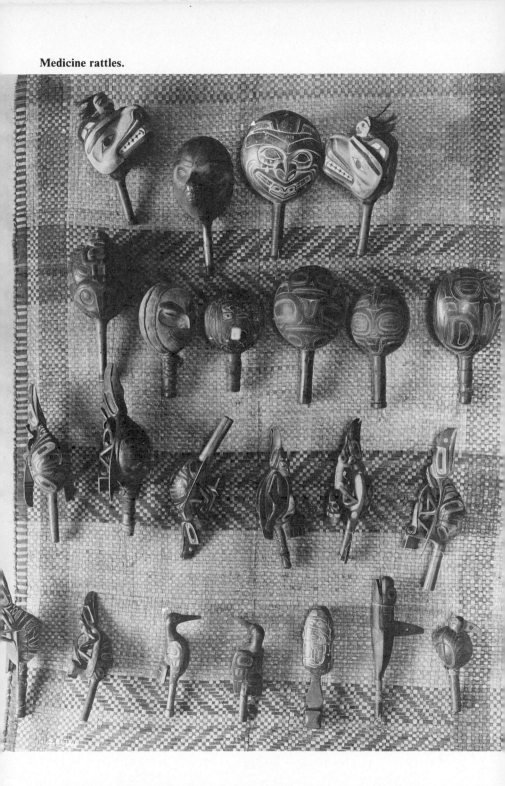

Wood Carving

Wooden rattle, in the shape of a bird.

Museum examples of wood carvers' skills from the past are either those made for the old culture and used in its daily life, or those made for sale to north coast visitors after about 1880, which, to be portable, were usually miniatures of Haida poles, house posts, canoes, boxes, bowls. We have very few names of carvers of the great full-sized poles, but Albert Edward Edenshaw, and Sam Qaoste and his son Peter Brown, were among them. Makers of small-scale poles and other wood carvings whose years spanned the nineteenth and twentieth centuries included Joshua Work, Luke Watson, George Smith, John Cross, Charles Gladstone and, of course, the famous Charles Edenshaw. Edenshaw made masks among other things, and his contemporaries Charles Gwaytihl and Daniel Stanley were also mask makers. The mask was one object that retained its size. Haida masks tended to be naturalistic, and those being made today follow that tendency.

A number of fine pieces are being produced in yellow and red cedar, from elaborate screens to small poles, bowls and dishes (sometimes inlaid with shell and bone) to masks and rattles. Power tools are used in the rough shaping, and the carver's choice of gouging blades are used in the refinement. Among the artists are Reid, Robert Davidson and his brother Reg Davidson, Freda Diesing, Alfred Collinson, and Steve Collison.

Haida masks.

Human face mask from Masset, dating from 1884.

National Museum of Canada, Ottawa
Neg. #102 121-F18

Shark mask, carved in alder by Robert Davidson. Photo: Reg Ashwell.

Argillite Carving

The raw material is a peculiar slate which the Haida quarry from a deposit high up Slatechuck Creek, northwest of Skidegate. Soft enough for carving, this dull gray-black slate can be transformed to a lustrous deep black by hand- and finger-rubbing. Argillite was probably carved for charms in pre-white times, and the most cerebral works in argillite, intricate panel pipes of Haida motif, may well have been used for ceremonial purposes; some were identified by professional collectors as "stone wands of doctors."

The earliest argillite carvings to show up in quantity, dating from 1818, took the form of pipes, with drilled stems and bowls. They may or may not have been used for smoking. Pipes reached ingenious complexity in the shape of horizontal panels up to forty centimeters long in which figures of legend were intertwined in frieze-like openwork. Panel pipes of "European-American" motif depicted ship decks and shipboard activities, complete with crewmen in lively postures; nothing like them exists elsewhere in the whole spectrum of northwest coast native art.

Haida artists of the nineteenth century also produced group and single figurines in argillite, significant as visual records of the days before the first photographs of Haida people; recorder-like instruments, bowls, plates and platters, ornate boxes, and a great many miniature poles. The best surviving examples in each category are incredibly beautiful. Inlays were sometimes used, the most desirable being dentalium (a mollusk) shell and California abalone shell.

Argillite carving of a steamer with floral motifs and manned by a white crew. Length: 10″.
Lowie Museum of Anthropology
University of California, Berkeley

Wilson Duff with Haida argillite chest.

Almost every Haida artist has carved in argillite; Charles Edenshaw used it to create some of his most spectacular work, and Bill Reid has produced memorable panel pipes, story poles, and jewelry. Rufus Moody has made argillite carving his career. In the last twenty years, young carvers led by Ron Wilson have ventured into free forms with notable success. Major traditional carvers of the first part of this century such as Tom Price, John Cross, Lewis Collinson, Henry and Arthur Moody, Paul Jones, William Dixon, George Smith, Charles Gladstone, John Marks, and Andrew Brown have modern counterparts in Pat Dixon, the Yeltatzie brothers, Douglas Wilson, Ed Russ, Alfred Collinson, Greg Lightbown, Norman Pryce, Denny Dixon, and others. Two exceptionally-talented argillite carvers who died young were Isaac Chapman, a contemporary of Charles Edenshaw, and Pat McGuire, whose sensitive style stimulated the art in the 1960s.

Miniature Haida pole.

Carving of maritime
officer, showing
attention paid to
details of dress.
Collected in
mid-1800s.

Department of Ethnology
National Museum of Denmark

Author Leslie Drew, Artist Doug Wilson, and Frank Drew

Haida argillite carvings.
National Museum of Canada, Ottawa
Neg. #88927

Jewelry

Silver bracelet.

The most familiar pieces are silver and gold bracelets, made from coins in the last century, then from gold biscuits when banks made them available, and most recently from small bars of silver and gold prepared by various agencies to the level of malleability required by the jewelers' trade. Haida craftsmen have long been in the forefront of this northwest coast art form, and Bill Reid carried it further, producing superb rings and engraved boxes of gold whose lids have surmounting figures also in gold.

In bracelets, the metal surface is engraved with one crest in a balanced presentation. Background spaces may be plain or cross-hatched. After engraving, the strip is carefully beaten into tubular shape to fit the wrist.

Charles Edenshaw made many wide, beautifully designed bracelets, and other bracelet makers of his period included John Cross, John Marks, the young Lewis Collinson, the Adams family, and Gladstone. Francis Williams and Robert Davidson are two of the leading artists today, and other skilled jewelry makers include Wayne Wilson, James McGuire, Ron Wilson, George Yeltatzie, Sharon Hitchcock Baker, and Nelson Cross.

The Haida jewelry maker also produces necklaces, brooches, pendants, earrings and cuff links in precious metals, many of fine design and execution.

Carved argillite brooch in shape of human

B.C. Provincial Museum, V'
Neg. #CPN 13885

Prints

Eagle design by Bill Reid.

In the last fifteen years, Haida designs for flat surfaces have been broadcast as never before through the medium of silk-screen prints in limited editions. The direct antecedents were tattoos and the designs painted in pigments on house boards and screens, and engraved on cedar boxes. The preferred Haida colors are red and black, with blue-green as an auxiliary color in the early days. The artist preparing original designs today often ventures into a circular format. Commercial firms generally do the printing and marketing.

Some of the most successful printmakers have been Bill Reid, Robert Davidson, Reg Davidson, Gerry Marks, Don Yeomans, Freda Diesing, Ron Wilson, and Francis Williams.

The burst of silk-screen printing seems to have stimulated interest in design, and may lead to exploration of other graphic art mediums.

Bent-box design by Robert Davidson.

Hand-weaving

Traditionally, hand-weaving has been a craft of Haida women. At one time, weaving of spruce root, the inner bark of young cedar trees, and other wood and grass fibers made a variety of garments, from cloaks to rain and dance hats, as well as baskets, mats, screens, wraps for canoe travel, and cordage, but gradually the repertoire dwindled to hat-making. All women took part in gathering and preparing the fibers and knew the weaving process—checker work and twilled plaiting. In basketry and hat-making, the emphasis has been on elegant simplicity, both in the weaving and the shape of the finished article. Basket shapes depended on the purpose: some were cylindrical; others were wallet shaped as in the case of twined spruce-root baskets which, when filled with stones, made anchors; some flat baskets were of mixed cedar bark and spruce root. In plain twined weave, baskets could be made watertight, but open work was also practiced. Early spruce-root baskets often had contrasting bands of roots dyed dark brown or black. For fineness in weaving, few objects in Indian basketry can compare with small Haida baskets woven from a species of grass.

Haida hat makers work with the hat on their knees, weaving the strands in increasing circles from the truncated crown to the wide brim. For waterproof hats of spruce root, the warp was of double-strand thickness and, in this respect, distinctly Haida. Designs were usually applied to the hats in skip-stitch or painted on.

In 1897, C.F. Newcombe watched two women making baskets at John Wesley's house at Skidegate. The women sat on the floor and each of the baskets hung on long cords from the ceiling, suspended bottom up with the warp strands dangling below the finished bases. The women were driving home the weft strands with bone implements made specifically for the job.

A few Haida hand-weavers like Florence Davidson, a daughter of Charles Edenshaw, and Nora Bellas make hats for sale to the public and for friends for Haida dancing. But of all the surviving arts, this is the one most in need of encouragement.

Haida weaver.

Haida baskets.

Woven Haida hat w
painted designs.

Woven Haida hat.

Haida basket.

Weaving a mat. Photo: C.F. Newcombe, 1902.
.C. Provincial Museum, Victoria

Conclusion

Haida art, as we have seen, has always been intimately
associated with Haida identity. Although the organized complexity
of the old culture can never be regained, in the Charlottes the Haida
can retain and, if they wish, reshape their identity as a people. This
will be the challenge to their artists of the future.